UNDERSTANDING REALITY

What is it to understand oneself in the fullest possible way? To explore in great depth what it is to be human. Is it possible to go beyond the existing foundations that have been laid within us by other human beings and strip away completely, all external influences that have shaped our thinking, literally resetting the operating system within our very own mind? Is it possible to act without thought of the environmental limitations embedded into us from birth?

The questions asked are perhaps beyond comprehension to answer, but this should not in itself be a limiting factor in the quest of truly knowing and understanding oneself.

An inexplicable drive to reach the absolute beginning, can bring a person to a place of total emptiness, not to be confused with loneliness or aloneness. Only then can one own the ability to step foot onto their very own path, a path that they choose in life, not a path directly or indirectly chosen for them.

Our body may never be free on this planet, but our mind can absolutely be liberated. The sense of control and power this brings is so profound and untouchable by any other being, that we then become fully capable of exploring our true purpose in life.

About the author

Named by his parents 'Benjamin Fail', the author is a person no more or less important than any other human.

Foreword

Each one of us has our own behavioural pattern that can be traced back to the environment in which we were raised. It is imperative for one to understand that these behavioural patterns are not set in stone, they can be adapted and even eliminated if the desire to do so exists.

This is by no means easy, but it is possible. Comprehension combined with an open and free mind can bring such vitality to life.

Fact: No one can change their past. **Reality:** No one has to allow their past to define who they are today.

———

When looking into a mirror,
Who do I see?
A mere illusion of consequence?
Or a soul longing to be free?

Fuelled from the past,
Exists great pain inside,
It will define me,
Should I choose to hide.

Lies great strength,
Within us all,
If not used wisely,
Is to erect a wall.

———

UNDERSTANDING REALITY

'Death smiles at us all, but all a man can do is smile back.' - M. Aurelius

The only certainty in life, is death. This is a fact and yet most people have no idea what it is they are meant to be doing prior to that eventuality.

We are all told what to do, how to act, how to think, even what to think pretty much from birth.

Do we have any control of our own life?

Do our thinking patterns and actions truly stem from our environment upbringing, as B.F. Skinner suggested, or are we driven by something deep within?

———————

'It is the mark of an educated mind to be able to entertain a thought without accepting it.' - Aristotle

It can be difficult to conceive that our fundamental belief systems are built on indoctrination, on nothing. It is a difficult thought to comprehend of course, that one may have wasted much time and energy on something completely worthless. It is therefore no doubt easier to pig-headedly continue along a flawed path, than it is to admit one's own gullibility.

Humans are gullible, it is one of our many flaws.

Many people innately rebel from indoctrination, much to the frustration of those around them. Many people feel different, like they do not fit in, like they do not belong, like they are drawn towards a purpose they have yet to discover. That feeling never leaves some people, they only get more adept at suppressing their true feelings in order to please others.

The reality is that although many believe they feel different, they in fact feel no different to most other people.

The 'one-size-fits-all' approach to life, is applicable to virtually no one with independence.

Do we create the lives we live, or do they create us?

A ship cannot travel to the other side of the globe in the blink of an eye, yet it can set a new course in an instant. This is applicable to humans and their lives, all it takes is courage.

———————

It is fear that limits people from reaching their very own unique potential.

A perpetual mundane existence will continue to cycle on generation after generation unless people wake up and act without fear.

We should never allow ourselves to be numbed and dumbed-down by the very society in which we inhabit.

———————

Discontentment with 'normality' and a capricious attitude to life is generally seen as a negative way to be.

It is suggested, often voluntarily, that we ought to be happy with our lives, happy to abide by 'the rules' and live a Sisyphic life.

The apparent consequences to such discontentment are those of one 'losing' what they apparently have. The reality is that nobody truly owns anything but their own life, of which is moving towards the end, from the very moment they are conceived.

Too much emphasis is placed on the material aspect of life, and little on anything else.

Only to death will we ever lose the people who are meant to be in our lives.

———

We are without doubt at our happiest when we are surrounded by the people we love. Communicating with them, without fear of judgment, and sharing our time with one another.

The misconception is that yearning for freedom and enlightenment bares reflection on the people we love, this is not true.

The freedom and enlightenment we seek, lies at the very centre of our lives, as though it runs through our very being. There is little comprehensible way of describing it, or what 'it' actually is, only that it exists inside of us all. And despite many peoples attempts to suppress it, including our own at times, it never leaves us. Ignorance is not bliss.

Unfortunately, many often influential people are bewildered by this, and so cast a negative energy towards any kind of dialogue in relation.

It is worth noting that sanity is purely subjective depending on what side of the 'asylum' one is standing.

———————

It is difficult to examine our purpose in life due to the way humans have set the system within the world we inhabit.

Money, possessions, power, and status within hierarchical systems are what humans have been conditioned and manipulated to believe is their purpose in life. This is no purpose, it is a trap.

The delicious looking apple that is rotten to the core. How can so many not see this?

Of course, it is not for one human to decide what is right or wrong for another human. However, we do have a moral obligation to our fellow human beings to question everything.

If a human fears questions, there is always a reason behind that fear.

It is by no means easy to establish one's purpose in life.

Perhaps a simpler way to figure out what one's purpose is, is to figure out what one's purpose is not.

Many times, people will falter and inevitably revert to their comfortable programmed state, and back to places mentally and physically 'cheap', unfulfilling, and shameful.

This vicious cycle can take one to a very deep and dark place, paralysed by feelings of inexplicable emotional agony, fear and guilt.

Physical pain is often very easy to treat by comparison to mental pain.

———————

Our system does not support the natural functioning of our minds. For example, it has been concluded that the answer to dealing with mental pain, is to subdue it via unnatural medication, rendering the personality flatlined. Alternatively, one can partake in cognitive behavioural therapy (CBT), administered by experts in theory.

So many humans are labelled 'depressed'.

Is it right to medicate and suppress a human because they feel dissatisfied and think differently to others?

Is it not simply that such humans are unaware of what it is they are really feeling inside themselves?

Could it possibly be the yearning for more than an artificial existence based around the shallow illusion of happiness, contentment, and desire?

Why is this artificial existence encouraged? How much money do the manufacturers and suppliers of this medication make? Do the suppliers have links with governments? How do they 'win' their contract to supply? Why are doctors so quick to diagnose 'depression' and medicate?

Many humans are imprisoned inside their own mind through fear. Fear that in reality does not exist.

Ironically, fear is mostly the creation of other humans', themselves full of fear, who freely offer their own voluntary analysis and observations of unconventionality.

———————

Too much weight is given to the interpretations and opinions of other human beings and their 'understanding' about our very own selves.

Many people gullibly believe that 'experts' understand our minds better than we do. Are we not our very own masters?

What right does one human have to analyse another human? Yet, we give way so easily to the opinions of others, especially those deemed 'qualified'.

Power and freedom will come only when we have faith in our own understanding of ourselves and seek not the approval of others.

A time existed, not so long ago, when humans truly believed that homosexuality was a psychological disorder, and as such it was stigmatised, making those people feel they had a problem simply because they did not think like the 'majority'.

If a person thinks and/or acts differently today, they have a similar stigma.

Tomorrow will show that today's understanding of 'mental health' was as incorrect as past thinking relating to homosexuality.

People are not having 'mental health' problems, they are going through a mental revolution, and medication is very seldom the answer.

Gaining an understanding of one's own mind in order to proceed is essential. Suppressing the internal revolution is absolutely the wrong thing to do.

People must embrace their state of wakefulness and desire to change, instead of fighting to suppress it.

People change, and trying to anchor oneself to a personality of yesterday, or the ideas of another as to how we ought to act, and what is acceptable, is unintelligent and will lead to life-long frustration, misery, and suffering.

Our routine is of the upmost importance, if we get that wrong, our health suffers. And if our health suffers, our happiness suffers.

Establishing a positive routine that includes sound nutrition, regular exercise and learning, rest, freedom to think, and most importantly, love and laughter, is key to health and happiness.

We must vehemently avoid negative routines that include poor diet, lack of exercise, inadequate rest, suppression of thought, ignorance, lack of love and laughter.

The above, both positive and negative, are by no means exhaustive lists.

———————

Many people are on the cusp of understanding their mind and need to realise that it is actually very simple. Unfortunately, it is we ourselves who overcomplicate things inside of it, leading us to feel lost.

The key is to simplify life, uncovering and rediscovering in order to learn and enjoy the beauty that was, still is, and can be.

It is important in knowing oneself to unlearn and strip away all useless knowledge.

Knowledge is not always power.

Correct knowledge is powerful.

Incorrect knowledge is a dangerous hindrance to a successfully happy life.

We must never conflict with our thoughts. We must allow them absolute freedom to go wherever they wish. Then, we will flourish.

———

'Do nothing which is of no use.' - M. Musashi

Two time wasting exercises…thinking about the past and thinking about the future, neither exist.

It is easy to become fixated on time. This is of great detriment to the mind and body, which must both be cared for very gently.

When on an aeroplane, we are told to put on our own oxygen masks first, prior to helping others. The reason is quite simply because we are of no use to anyone else if we cannot function properly ourselves.

'If you are saying something that almost anyone else could say, then it's likely to be cliché or ideological. Whereas, if you are speaking from yourself, then in some sense you are the only person who could be saying that, and so what that means in some sense is that you have taken ideas, philosophical, even ideological, and you've made them personal, so that you are speaking from a position that only you can speak from, and then you have something original to offer....If you can predict what someone is going to say, on the basis of their set of beliefs, then they're not speaking, the ideology is speaking, and if the ideology is speaking, you don't even have to listen to them, you can just read about the ideology and make up your own mind.' – J. B. Peterson

Do we really understand how to think, or do we habitually think using ingrained patterns?

Can we think completely objectively? Is this possible?

Can we cease to think? Is that possible?

As always, things appear impossible until we achieve them.

Things may perhaps be extremely difficult, but very little is impossible.

It all begins with an acute awareness within the mind.

Am I aware that I am thinking? Am I aware that my thoughts are not entirely my own, but instead, mere adaptations of another's thoughts? Am I able to formulate my own thoughts? Dare I formulate my own thoughts? Do I have the courage to share my own thoughts? Dare I explore my own thoughts?

———————

Human obsession with tribalism is futile, and an immense waste of time and energy. Its sole purpose is to segregate and try to preserve a way of life that existed yesterday.

The foundation underpinning any tribe, is power.

The modern phenomenon of placing the word 'progressive' in front of things that are in no way progressive i.e. nationalism, conservatism, etc, is nothing more than an oxymoron.

The desire to fit into a tribe, appears to give many humans purpose, a sense of meaning, belonging, hope and security.

Why? What is this insatiable need to be wanted, validated, and owned? It stems from low self-esteem and fear.

True global peace and harmony can never exist as long as tribalism exists.

Are we not indigenous to Earth? To our solar system? To our galaxy? Our universe? How can humans get so passionate about a piece of land, or a religion that they happened to leave the womb and arrive into, with no choice of their own, by sheer accident of birth?

People will choose their friends, tribes and even life mates based on this chance of birth. They will argue, fight, and even die for one cause or another, primarily based on where they happened to be born or where their religious group is flourishing. Is this not insanity?

Surely this is so obviously a counterproductive and unintelligent way to behave?

'The first man who, having fenced in a piece of land, said 'This is mine', and found people naïve enough to believe him, that man was the true founder of civil society. From how many crimes, wars, and murders, from how many horrors and misfortunes might not any one have saved mankind, by pulling up the stakes, or filling up the ditch, and crying to his fellows: Beware of listening to this impostor; you are undone if you once forget that the fruits of the earth belong to us all, and the earth itself to nobody.' - Rousseau

Tribes can only function through dependency of herd mentality. Leaders, all very adept in the art of manipulation, market such nonsense and unfortunately, people buy so easily into it. It is wrong and an incredibly unintelligent way for humans to live. Many humans allow themselves to be submissively manipulated so easily, with little to no resistance, by so few. Why?

All forms of tribalism: Religion, nationalism, sport, political, age, race, gender, sexuality, philosophical, etc, are morally repugnant methods of control and serve no other purpose other than to create division and separation which inherently leads to conflict. Only after the total eradication of tribalism, will humans and all other life forms, begin to live, love, and respect each other.

A human is a human, and not a single one is worth more or less than another.

Do we think that by giving allegiance to a tribe, whatever it calls itself, it will be of any use to humanity?

What is the desire for humans to act in such an insecure and selfish way?

If tribes exist, peace cannot.

If one truly uses common sense, they will realise that the origins of all tribes can be traced back to one thing...a manipulative power thirsty human.

It can of course, be extremely difficult for many who have been indoctrinated from birth into functioning with a tribalistic mentality, to overcome their engrained and flawed belief system.

The only way to address this is by studying oneself and developing an awareness of any ingrained thought pattern and then quite simply, changing it.

'In individuals, insanity is rare; but in groups, parties, nations and epochs, it is the rule.' - F. Nietzsche

What is family? Is it to be linked through blood? Is it loyalty? Is it sharing a home? Do we even understand what a family is? What if humans thought of themselves as one family, the human family? What would the world look like if that were to happen?

Must a family have children? If they have children, whose responsibility is it to ensure that those children are loved, cared for, educated, and raised to become responsible, independent, loving, and happy humans?

Our homes are not all that dissimilar to a bird's nest. Once children are capable of 'flying from the nest', they should do so. They should explore the mental, physical, and heart felt realms of the world (and perhaps beyond). But they must be equipped to do so, and that comes from adequate parenting.

The parents of today are responsible for tomorrow's world.

All loving parents naturally want their children to be happy and really live, not merely exist. Unfortunately, a cold and clinical way of life exists whereby humans are manipulated to fall in line, barely able to think for themselves.

Of course, this is likely the way humans have been from the very beginning, and it quite possibly isn't a modern phenomenon.

But what is it like to be a child today? Under the microscope constantly. Treated as though a candidate for life.

People who talk down to children must never be tolerated.

Adults can learn a lot from children if they bother to really listen instead of pacifying them with technology and sugar.

The innocence of youth is such a gift and must be preserved throughout life.

'The idea is to die young as late as possible' – A. Montagu

Many adults have forgotten what it was like to be a child.

The way an adult treats a child is a reflection on how they were raised themselves.

Why become a teacher if you have little time for children?

Why become a parent if you are not prepared to commit fully to your child?

———

What is offence? What is it to be offended? Why are some humans easily offended by other humans? Are the former the result of a mollycoddled upbringing? Are the latter the result of a hard up bringing? Why would a human wish to directly offend another human? Are easily offended humans' mere narcissists? Observe and question this.

If a clown has no audience, will they still perform?

How can humans develop if they are hesitant to speak their thoughts in fear of upsetting another? Discussion and debate are positive and should never be suppressed.

Cowardice is a dreadful trait and humans who are afraid to speak their thoughts ought to ask themselves 'why?'.

Suppression of speech is social regression.

There is a difference of course between stirring up hatred and a person's right to speak freely. It comes down to using that very uncommon 'common' sense.

Should humans tolerate offence? Should they revolt?

Offence is a mere matter of perspective; the narrower the mind, the smaller the perspective, the more offended a person will be. The broader the mind, the more perspective, the less offended a person will be.

Is it possible for a human to say a single sentence without offending someone in the world?

———————

It is so easy to give more weight to what others say and do rather than to our own thoughts and actions.

Why do we watch and observe each other so much? Are we watching to learn? To admire? To worship? To offend? To control? Are we watching to live our lives through others? Or are we simply watching?

———————

Do we know who we are and what we want? Do we need others to tell us what we want and need? Must we depend on praise and acceptance?

Most people dislike hearing the truth and so opt not to listen. This of course does not mean that the truth does not exists.

It is very easy to fall into an array of diverse methods to spare hearing and admitting the truth.

Surrounding ourselves with 'yes' people who tell us what we want to hear is a mere illusion and of no benefit at all. It only serves to give the false idea that we do not have to take as much responsibility for the choices we make. It makes it easy should things go wrong, for the self-talk to be along the lines of: 'well this person/these people who I really respect, thought it was a good idea and advised me, so...'. This is a big mistake hugely detrimental to self-esteem and self-empowerment.

It is very common to point out flaws in other people, but self-development can only occur when we turn our awareness inwardly and analyse ourselves, honestly and individually. In this respect, it is imperative never to seek the opinion or validation of another, especially a friend or family member, as they will almost always give false praise and massage the ego that exists inside us all, to varying extents.

Most people are always going to be friendly and interested as long as something is being done for them or their cause. The second that changes, these types of people withdraw their friendship.

It can be a very hard lesson to trust and confide in the wrong person(s).

Nevertheless, a lesson learned is a blessing.

Never make the same mistake twice.

———————

Pleasure is necessary.

However, for some reason, pleasure is seen by many as a reward that ought to be earned first. Why?

Most people work all their life to 'enjoy' their short retirement. Is this intelligent?

Society has been encouraged to believe that working hard all week, then to enjoy a weekend is a dignified and honourable way to live.

It appears okay for us to have some pleasure, but not too much. And we are expected to be grateful for such reward with little complaint, for giving ourselves to the system and being 'good' hard-working people. This is a brainwashed existence.

Pleasure is a fundamental part of a 'successful' life.

A good indicator of success is how much a person smiles, laughs, loves and is happy, rather than their bank balance and/or their status.

For sure, people can get pleasure and purpose from work, but there is no comparison to the pleasure and purpose one gets from love.

If a person only feels great purpose and pleasure solely from their work, then that person is a very sad person who is completely wasting their life, and will, as is so often the case, realise it once it is too late.

Many views of pleasure stem from religion, both directly and indirectly.

The idea that pleasure is to be limited and earned through some pre-suffering, comes from religion.

Religions are nothing more than methods of manipulative control.

———————

Humans are inherent followers, striving to 'fit in' to a well disguised slavish existence and be accepted. Money and status both play a big part in this need for acceptance.

We may never truly be free in this world in a physical sense, but the same cannot be said regarding our mental state.

Is it possible for a person to free themselves from the engrained and embedded prejudices bestowed upon us from birth?

Only with an awareness to see with clarity and honesty, will we be free.

———

The only real currency worth spending, is time.

Time to connect, to love, and to live equally alongside people and nature, not with something non-existent.

The irony is that things of little value are usually tangible. Yet things that generally mean the most, do not exist in a physical sense. On the surface this is a strange statement, as we can touch people. However, it is not a person's physicality that makes them who they are, it is their spirit, soul, and heart. This is very evident when one sees a person so beautiful that lacks spirit, soul, and heart, as behind their superficial beauty, they are usually always cold, uninteresting, and somewhat ugly people.

———————

The connection between the body and mind in its simplest form is that the mind thinks, and the body feels. To upset the balance and solely think, or solely feel, will lead to suffering.

To overthink leads to loneliness, to over feel leads to emotional ruin. To do neither is to simply exist.

One must never allow their thoughts to control their feelings, nor their feelings to control their thoughts.

Our thoughts and feelings are at the very essence of what make us human.

If one can align both the body and mind harmoniously, they can enjoy real love, happiness, and contentment.

It is possible to step back from the memories of yesterday and the thoughts of tomorrow and sever all ties with the ever so common self-fulfilling prophecy of anxiety and depression.

The past is good at telling us who we are and where we came from, but it is a terrible indicator of where we can go and who we can become.

One must never be a slave to the past, as no good ever comes of that type of thinking. People who are slaves to their past are always unhappy people. It is imperative to stop thinking about the past.

The future does not exist, so there is no point wasting words on that. We only have the now, today, this second.

One thing that is certain, as Lou Tice said, is that *'We move towards, and become like, that which we think about. Our present thoughts determine our future.'*

Thinking miserably and negatively today will for sure lead to a negative, miserable, and lonely tomorrow.

Allowing past based thoughts to flourish, will result in a life going nowhere.

One must be positive, with a continuous renewed freshness of thought and action.

'Happiness consists in activity. It is a running stream, not a stagnant pool.' – J. M. Good

———————

When born, it is reasonable to suggest that our only two innate behaviours, are unhappiness; which can be witnessed in the form of crying and irritability, and happiness; which can be witnessed in the form of laughter and positive movement.

It could therefore be argued that all fears are purely environmental. The presence of fear in a child's environment is very easily absorbed and will remain well into adulthood, more often than not, lasting an entire lifetime.

People who experience fear as a child, are highly likely to hold many negative traits such as, over sensitivity, hyper emotional, secrecy, hatred, selfishness, paranoia, insecurity, jealousy, self-consciousness, coldness, greed, low self-esteem, loneliness, egotism, etc...

Adult humans like comfortable questions yet dislike uncomfortable questions.

People are often so easily offended if they do not receive the answers they expect.

People often feel uncomfortable asking certain questions.

Fear of the truth is to accept the life of a lie. And to accept the life of a lie, is weak.

Fear, manipulation, power, deception, control, money, etc... breeds a secretive mindset.

'Secrecy is the badge of fraud' – Sir J. Chadwick

Everybody is struck with fear at some point in their lives, but it is how we deal with fear that defines and shapes us.

Never accept fear. Face it head-on and eliminate its underlying cause.

Fear has fear of transparency and truth.

———————

Many people understandably contemplate suicide.

It can make one feel uncomfortable and embarrassed to think about how close they have come.

The feeling of being so incredibly lost and in the darkest depths of inner 'hell', is no place to loiter.

To decide to live, is a choice.

To decide to live but not as before, is a choice.

Every day a suicidal person continues to live, is like free time to them. Time they would not have had if they had killed themself. There is a certain freedom to this way of thinking and acting.

What is the worst life can throw at us?

Is anything worth ending this beautiful life for?

The reason many seek the homemade noose, is fear. Fear to be themselves.

One must get comfortable being uncomfortable. This is positive.

Whether we are different to those around us or not, it is irrelevant.

Uncontrolled fear can bring feelings unexplainable paralysis.

Let go of fear, completely.

'I rebel; therefore I exist.' - A. Camus

———————

One of the root causes of 'depression' is a negative routine.

Humans need a basic routine in life...eat, sleep, activity...but it is what we do and how we think in between that gives us purpose, or lack of.

Purpose is what keeps our sanity intact.

Love is purpose.

Do we want to know ourselves properly and explore our capabilities? If so, we must fear nothing, no fear of failure, or of judgment, etc, but fear of absolutely nothing.

Fear is a terrible trait, environmentally engrained upon a person. It has no place alongside love.

One must be aware that 'love' as in the mere thought of the word love, can fuel fear.

A person may think they are in love, however, should they experience jealousy, control, aggression, fear of losing, or any other insecurity, they do not understand love and are confusing it with something else.

Falling in love with a person who does not understand love, or worse still, they do understand it but use it to manipulate, will lead to immense suffering both mentally and physically. As difficult as it may be, such a person must be completely cut out of one's life, as they will only ever serve to administer great pain hidden behind the falseness of the mere words 'I love you'.

The power of fear can be that of a 'wolf in sheep's clothing' with regards to love.

Love and fear cannot exist together.

With love exists no fear, and with fear exists no love.

———————

People waste time and effort focusing on irrelevance.

Passion and enthusiasm are given in abundance to a myriad of superficial topics such as judgement.

Irrational reaction to judgment passed by another human is demeaning and extremely limiting to one's own wellbeing.

It is difficult for many people to see that it is their own reaction itself that serves to feed the judgment in the first instance. It is the law of supply and demand.

It is true that narrow minds cast judgment all too easily. However, good and bad, right and wrong are subjective, and so people must never allow judgment to have any effect on them whatsoever.

Unfortunately, people allow themselves to be guided through the judgment and opinions of others. The result, they conform, acting powerlessly in an almost robotic fashion.

———————

To evolve, one must have a balanced mindset of addition and subtraction. Adding value (not financially) and subtracting unnecessary mundane nonsense.

If the balance is lost, unhappiness follows.

———————

Humans have an intriguingly illogical way about them, placing their trust in other human beings in the name of 'politics'. The idea being that these humans (politicians) will represent their 'interests'. However, the reality is that 'people' become subordinate to politicians, who so frequently represent their own interests, or the interests of the tribe they represent. This perpetual cycle has little to no value, and one must resist the temptation to get involved in such futility.

If true progress is to be made, if even possible at all, humans must communicate with much more efficiency, transparency and willingness to listen and learn on a global scale, and without the absolute necessity to do so via politicians.

Humans have been communicating with one another since the beginning of their existence, and today as we know, humans enjoy communicative abilities on an unprecedented level, yet we still think and act so narrowly on a tribalistic and monetary scale. Why not organise and communicate with our human family on a global and humanitarian scale? This would be true positive progress.

———————

Love is the essence of human existence, not conflict.

What good has ever resulted from conflict or war?

People are more important than any status, title, or any wealth a minority of people possess.

The majority are being led and controlled by the minority, the 'ruling class'.

No 'class' should exist other than the human class.

———————

Mental suffering is difficult to eradicate, but it is by no means impossible. The key lies in finding purpose.

Physical suffering on the other hand, is very straight forward and easy to eradicate. If humans would communicate and think together, such unnecessary suffering, for example, starvation, sexual abuse, etc, would not exist in the world.

How can one harm another for self-gratification? Retribution must be sought on humans who act in such vile ways of hatred and disgust, partaking in heinous crimes. These people must be shown the full capability of human vengeance.

Our magnificent world has much beauty but also unfortunately much unnecessary suffering.

How can love prevail when there exists sex trafficking, for example?

For humanity to progress, we must not suppress our innate sense of justice/injustice.

Depths of retaliatory aggression exist in us all and must not to be suppressed.

Strength to act lies inside of us all and we must not tolerate and turn a blind eye to any terrible crimes being brought against and humans, vulnerable or not, that we coexist with.

Sex trafficking and paedophilia are but two very real attacks against humanity.

What does it say about us if we tolerate its very existence? How can such a successful evil prevail in such a beautiful world? The answer is simple, it is because we have allowed it to do so. Because there is no monetary value in helping such humans to live. And because the problem goes to the very highest levels of the ruling class.

Every single disgusting human involved in such atrocity, must be unrelentingly hunted and dealt with in the most severe manner.

'It is better to be violent, if there is violence in our hearts, than to put on the cloak of non-violence to cover impotence.' - M. Gandhi

Humans that prey on weaker humans deserve no place in life. Within us exists the balance of great love and great hatred. This hatred must be summoned, when necessary, to the protection of people in need, and of love.

———

It is extremely easy for our actions to become mere reactions to other humans' dogmatic beliefs, slipping without resistance into an easy life of conformity through fear of standing alone.

Many people so willingly accept what they are told by other humans, especially those humans who have positioned themselves within some man-made hierarchical structure.

People can never be free to think independently or let their own actions evolve as long as they are content to follow and be spoon-fed 'information' and 'knowledge' from their 'masters'.

One must trust in their own thoughts and feelings, free from external influence and/or fear of conflict, and strive with unwavering resolve and determination to explore, experience, and enjoy the only life they are going to get, to its absolute fullest.

We must strip away every single one of our fears and make ourselves immune to outside pressures and expectations.

We require no validation from any other human being.

This requires a great study of our very own individual history, not to be confused with the study of any other human, but the study of the self. Not simply pruning but rather getting to the root of who we are and why we think and acts the way we do. Only then, after deep and honest self-analysis, can we begin to travel along our very own unique and fulfilling path with such clarity.

———————

It is important to have belief in one's own capabilities and dispel all external opinions and expectations. This can only be achieved, first and foremost, with an acute awareness of the subversive oppressor. These people come individually and/or in groups. Their actions can be both conscious and unconscious. They can be friends, acquaintances, or enemies. Perhaps the hardest to spot are the family members and friends who unconsciously and unintentionally oppress. We are most likely to give sanction to their opinions and beliefs with little to no resistance.

———

'Whenever you find yourself on the side of the majority, it is time to pause and reflect.' - M. Twain

Despite many people being content to build and develop their thoughts and lives on top of other people's foundations, it is possible to build one's own life structure based on one's very own and unique foundations.

What makes those that went before us, right? or indeed wrong? What if a person spends their entire life following another person's philosophy, unchallenged? Is this intelligent?

We must always question in great depth when laying our foundations, as that is precisely what they are, OUR foundations. If we get these wrong, the whole structure of our beliefs, behaviours and entire life will be majorly flawed and the realisation will come crashing down at some point, it is simply a matter of time.

———————

'Intelligent people tend to have less friends than the average person. The smarter you are, the more selective you become.' – N. Tesla

What does it mean to be intelligent? A huge misconception is that intelligence goes hand-in-hand with academia. Academics are people just like non-academics and do not automatically qualify as intelligent. Intelligence goes beyond education.

Are narrow minded people, intelligent? Are people who follow others, intelligent? Are obedient people, intelligent? Are submissive people, intelligent? Are dominating people, intelligent? Are people who put work before love, intelligent? Are people who mistreat themselves, intelligent? Are people who mistreat others, intelligent? Are people who waste their life, intelligent? Are people who live in the past or the future, intelligent? Are people who cannot take responsibility, intelligent? Are people who do not have the ability to listen, intelligent? Are judgmental people, intelligent? Are people who think they are indispensable, intelligent? Are people who do things they would rather not do, intelligent? Are people who hurt the ones they love, yet show respect to the ones they do not love, intelligent?

Intelligent people are creative people, not followers. They do not simply re-write and/or re-invent other people's work.

Imitation may be the highest form of flattery; however, it bears little relation to intelligence. Unless of course, the individual is imitating in order to flatter and further themselves through manipulation, hiding their own lack of understanding and knowledge. This is common, and in a way, could be argued is intelligent. Not morally sound, nevertheless, intelligent.

An intelligent person has the mind/body balance talked about earlier, understanding very clearly the necessity in aligning thoughts with feelings and not suppressing either to the detriment of the other.

'A sane person to an insane society must appear insane.' - K. Vonnegut

———————

Sleep is perhaps the easiest way of crossing over fully from body to mind.

Do we want to sleep alone? Do we want to sleep beside a person while thinking about another?

Constant chattering within the mind coupled with deafening silence ringing in the ears leads many adults to insomnia.

Overstimulation and lack of control within the brain leads to nonstop thoughts of everything but one's present reality. One must let go and be in the present.

Adequate and high-quality sleep is one of the fundamentals to a happy life.

Always sleep beside the right person of whom the upmost connection and unity is held with.

———————

Our modern system has people in such a hurry to get some place they would really rather not be. Why? If humans really took the time to appreciate the beauty of life and the planet they inhabit, they would be more apt to care for it and its inhabitants (including themselves).

The whole 'just keep moving forward' philosophy is only beneficial if indeed we are moving in the right direction.

What is the right direction?

The right direction is the direction that each and every one of us know inside to be true. This is only applicable personally. The moment another human presses their own opinion as to the direction one ought to be going, is the moment one ought to create some distance from that human, because consciously or unconsciously, they are limiting to that person's progress and happiness.

Many people rarely get to where they want.

Most that do, realise that it is not what they thought, or where they want to be, and so they move on to another destination.

It is an unfortunate perpetual cycle that is very common, leading to a complete waste of life.

Do we know how to relax? Do we know how to just stop? How to take a moment and realise what we have?

Constantly seeking something that does not exist is a complete waste of life.

Is it intelligent to waste a life?

Allowing ourselves time to re-balance, evaluate, and rejuvenate, is of high importance if we are to remain happy and healthy.

It is unfortunate that relaxation is seen and portrayed as a 'lazy' activity.

The fact that relaxation gives a person 'development time', time to realise what is important, and prioritise, time to cut out all the useless nonsense and really declutter their life, is discouraged in our system of living.

To advocate and promote the positive significance of thinking, would cause great problems to those wishing to continue to dominate, manipulate, and rule.

One must make guilt-free time to relax, as it is fundamental to happiness.

———————

Humans frequently mistake lust for love. Sexual experiences and adrenaline rushes are extremely addictive and can quickly become a necessity and intern, a big problem. Love is a whole different experience.

Of course, lust and love are not merely confined to people, intimately speaking.

One of the most lustful things in life, is power. Can one love power? Is it possible to love power? What is power? Is it not simply another word for control? Can one love control? Many can certainly lust over control. What is control? Does control exist without approval? How does one gain approval to control another person and/or group of people? Manipulation?

For person 'a' to control person 'b', or group 'a' to control group 'b', then 'a' must gain the approval of 'b' to do so.

Is it intelligent to willingly give approval to be controlled by another(s)?

If one finds oneself in a man-made hierarchical position, and asks simply 'why did I (perhaps still do) give my approval, willingly, to be manipulated and controlled by another(s)?', what would their answer be?

Why do so many humans respect authority so much?

Why do so many humans believe other humans to know what is best for them? The answer, low self-esteem.

———————

Love is a powerful and uncontrollable force? According to Plato, love is 'a serious mental disease'. Anyone who proclaims or supports such a statement clearly does not understand love, and very likely has never experienced it.

Those who have experienced love, they will know and understand its very positive power. The constant energy it brings, along with the most remarkable and indescribable feelings of happiness, warmth, contentment, loyalty, bliss, and security.

Anyone who has felt love, would never describe it negatively.

Selfish people can never live harmoniously with love.

'Everything has its beauty, but not everyone sees it.' - Confucius

Love is happiness and happiness is love.

Hate is misery. Why waste a second on hate when time is so precious?

Life is better when filled with love.

love is the 'skeleton key' to life.

One can have all the tangible riches in existence, but if not love, life is meaningless.

———————

Never watch life from the side lines. Participate, never spectate.

'Maybe it's not about the length of time you've known someone; maybe it's about instant recognition on an unconscious level. Our souls know each other' – S.E. Hall

Many people appear to form connections easily with other people but never really connect with them.

If it is difficult to relax and be totally open around a person, regardless of whether they think and behave differently, the connection is weak.

Keeping a connection with a manipulative person must be avoided at all costs.

If one can feel completely 100% at ease in another person's company, a strong connection exists. This must not be mistaken to mean a conflict of opinion will never arise. On the contrary, truly connected people argue much more than weakly connected people. They challenge each other's views and opinions but always have total respect for one another.

———————

Never waste time observing futility.

Never waste time observing observers.

Never fear connection.

It is possible to be attached to another person and feel little to no connection. Most people experience this out of convenience. Such a connection is not rewarding or nurturing in the slightest.

Never bury feelings, always addressed them head on.

Connecting with a wonderful person of such depth, dignity, and warmth, is a feeling like no other.

————

The profoundness of her mind,
speech so delicately spoken,
she may not know how I look at her,
or the feelings she has awoken.

Skin as perfect as the clearest sky,
smile as pure as her heart,
a definite moment shared together,
in this life, must we always remain apart?

———————

'Do not spoil what you have by desiring what you have not; remember that what you now have was once among the things you only hoped for.' - Epicurus

Striving for more is a good or bad thing depending on what the 'more' is.

To strive for more superficial unnecessary possessions is bad for sure. But to strive for more knowledge and understanding of oneself, or to strive for love and intern, happiness, is very good.

The trap to avoid, in striving for a more positive life, is pushing away the very people that we love, who make us happy. This is counterproductive and leads only towards misery.

We often place ultimatums upon ourselves, 'it is either this or that, not both', this is a very unintelligent way to approach life.

It is unnecessary to suffer in order to enjoy life.

It is possible to be happy, content, and in-love, and do the right things without causing internal or external conflict.

It is fear of the external conflict that holds many humans back from living the life that would bring them true happiness, contentment, and love.

Unfortunately, there is no fail-safe method of identifying the people who are for and against our success.

People who are genuinely supportive and positive are rare. Unfortunately, the same cannot be said of those ever so common people who bring negativity to life. The latter of whom are extremely dangerous to anyone wishing to live a rich and full life of love and happiness.

Wherever possible, negatively charged people must be dismissed from any significant role of one's life.

Health is wealth.

Happiness is health.

Love is happiness.

Love is wealth.

Love is life.

———————

The materialistic human who places great importance on material possessions, money and status is the sad and lonely human.

———————

'Tis better to have loved and lost than never to have loved at all.' -
A. Tennyson

Soon we go our separate ways,
Our hearts they fill with sorrow,
Take solace in the sense of happiness,
For we are sure to meet again tomorrow.

The passing of a loved one is an awful experience but inevitable.

Only a human devoid of love will escape this experience.

————————

Only the awake person can see what is truly important in life.

———————

'When one loses the deep intimate relationship with nature, then temples, mosques and churches become important.' - J. Krishnamurti

Unless we can understand ourselves, we are nothing more than socially lobotomised carcasses who unquestionably and so willingly follow the trail of manipulative garbage peddled and pushed by those who are motivated to control.

———————

'How fortunate for governments that the people they administer don't think.' - A. Hitler

Politics is pointless if it does not serve beneficially to all people.

Happiness and contentment cannot exist if even the smallest of minorities are forgotten about or mistreated. Any such unfortunate minority has absolutely the right to rebel and revolt.

Extremism aside, generally political theory it is good. Unfortunately, the practice seldom translates the theory.

With more educated people today than likely ever before, it is astounding that so many with no common sense or courage, end up in politics. People willing to do whatever it takes in order to fulfil their own selfish interests.

The few controlling the masses with no change ever taking place.

Would humans democratically elect a person with no prior experience, training, or education to be a surgeon or an aeroplane pilot for example? Would such people be successful or bring confidence to anyone relying on them? Why is it accepted to democratically elect people with little to no experience, training, or expertise to be leaders and law makers of a country?

Perhaps there is a better way.

———

Advice often flows freely from the people with nothing original to
say.

'You may never know what results come of your actions, but if you do nothing, there will be no results.' - M. Gandhi

Idleness is a waste of life, a mind killer.

Humans can be active whilst being idle, they can also be inactive whilst being busy.

To be idle is to be nothing.

Procrastination leads to suffering and regret.

Do what needs to be done and do it with passion, or do not do it at all.

———

'Music is indeed the mediator between the spiritual and the sensual life.' – L. Van Beethoven

Music is very powerful and magical, and has the ability to invoke immense feelings of passion and heightened senses.

Beware poor grade music, as it is detrimental to mental and physical health.

Much like love, music is a soul cleanser.

Time must be afforded to music.

———————

'But still try for who knows what is possible!' - M. Faraday

Too much time is spent thinking of negative ideas as to why very real positives will fail.

A negative mind is a scared and scarred mind that unfortunately leads to a negative life of blame.

———

Never allow the mood of another to determine your own mood. This is common behaviour unfortunately, but who really wants to be common?

Unless of course humanity can get to the point of total happiness, only then could one be content to be common.

Common happiness is a truly wonderful thought.

A smile naturally feels better than a frown.

A smile releases more positive energy than a frown.

They key lies in finding the cause of one's smile and then unashamedly making that cause a priority.

'A simple smile. That's the start of opening your heart and being compassionate to others.' – Dalai Lama

———————

Toxic people can drain the life out of anyone. Playing the victim constantly, they generally convince themselves more than they ever convince anyone else.

One must always remember that when dealing with a toxic person, it is no one's fault.

Toxic people have an unfortunate sickness within them, and so any argument with them is very simply unfair and wrong. Only a coward would choose to argue with a sick person.

It is important to understand that no matter how hard one tries to help a toxic person, they will always play the victim, seeing any helper as a perpetrator.

The most beneficial thing anyone can do when dealing with a toxic person, is to cut them off.

They have the same unfortunate issue that a drug addict does, they simply cannot be helped until they themselves decide to open up honestly and seek help.

Unfortunately, they rarely realise their own situation. The world is their problem, and their very existence causes them pain. It is extremely sad of course, but nevertheless true.

Toxic people find it difficult to love and will frequently cause hurt to those who love them.

Their problems stem from childhood.

If a person tries to remain close to a toxic person out of pity, it will be as though two people fell out of a boat into the ocean, one person can swim and the other cannot. The person who cannot swim will panic so much that they will hold onto the other. Eventually, both will drown.

———————

Thought provocation is good.

Thought suppression is bad.

We must beware those who try to dominate our thoughts, never being submissive of mind or giving way to any form of manipulation.

Once a person and/or a group controls our thoughts, they control us.

We must trust ourselves and our own intuitive feelings, and fiercely resist those who seek to control.

'At 70 years old, if I could give my younger self one piece of advice, it would be to use the words "fuck off" much more frequently.' – H. Mirren

———————

Being completely honest is one of the most difficult things to do in life. It is much easier to live a lie.

Lies are a form defence, they hide and protect the real 'you'.

Lies are directly related to lack of courage and weakness, born out of fear.

If we were completely honest with ourselves, where would we be today? Who would we be with? What would we be doing?

To willingly expose one's own honest feelings, takes great courage and mental strength.

Lies will haunt a person their entire life.

To lie to another can be justified at times of course, but one should never lie to themselves nor to the one(s) they love.

Lying to a loved one(s) can never be justified.

Love and lies can never exist together.

Which is more important, the love or the lie?

———————

Beware ideologues for they have little to no mind or voice of their own.

These people are extremely easy to spot as they are advocates of group identity and almost always speak and seek to promote their groups manipulative ideology.

They are not intelligent people. Mere hypnotised puppets.

Ideologues are manipulated to thoughtfully suppress their own feelings and actively encourage others to do the same.

Never succumb to an ideologue's sophist justification for their apparent noble cause.

———

How happy can a person make their life?

It is a certainty that no one can enjoy a happy life while always focusing on negativity.

Caring about problems enough to want to help is of course a good thing to do, but not to the detriment of one's own life. That might sound selfish, but rest assured it is not.

If your life is happy, you will positively affect those around you with happiness. A smile and laughter are extremely infectious.

Energy flows, and so why not allow that energy to be positive energy?

No matter what we do, the type of energy we use shows. For example, how we speak to one another, how we treat one another, even how we make food, etc…all so much better when partaken with positive energy.

People in love are very easy to spot as they radiate positive energy.

Miserable lonely cold people are even easier to spot as they radiate heavy and negative energy.

Never allow negativity to trump positivity.

Negativity can consume and ruin a life and the lives of those close by.

———————

Is the purpose of life to waste life? Is it to do as we are told? Is it to conform? Is it to see how much money we can accrue? Is it to see how high up the man-made hierarchy we can get? Is it to chase the validation of others? Is it to chase a rank or title, or see how many letters or numbers we can get before or after our name? Is it to work for someone or have someone work for us? Is it to see how many people we can get to like us? Is it to be superficial? Is it to submit oneself to others?

———————

'Kindness is the language which the deaf can hear and the blind can see' – M. Twain

Do not strive to be benevolent, be benevolent.

———————

Do we need to be controlled and accepted?

Why would any intelligent person allow rules formed by others, to govern their happiness?

This unhealthy behaviour stems from past-born fear.

Unfortunately, if not addressed directly and honestly, fear will continue to control and rule within, growing stronger as time passes.

Fear is mere habit.

Addressing issues from the past is essential if one wishes to be happy and healthy today.

It comes down to a choice, does a person allow themselves to continue to be enslaved by their own past or by those around them, or do they take charge of themselves and simply say 'No! No more! I am done behaving this way! From this second onward, I no longer behave this way.'?

'In the long run, we shape our lives, and we shape ourselves. The process never ends until we die. And the choices we make are ultimately our own responsibility.' – E. Roosevelt

'When we blindly adopt a religion, a political system, a literary dogma, we become automatons. We cease to grow.' - A. Nin

Why do humans allow themselves to give way to other humans? Who rightfully has superiority over another? Why do we conform so willingly? Why do we relinquish ourselves to dogma? Where does this lack of self-belief come from? Have we become so conditioned from birth, that our reticular activating system is now on autopilot? Is it possible to 'hack' into this system and regain manual control of our minds? Are antidepressants a way of ensuring the human consciousness remains remote controllable?

Are antidepressants and psychological counselling human methods of dealing with things they have little to no comprehension of? Fear of the unknown and fear to change often scares people so much that they resist, opting instead to maintain their own unhealthy status quo.

For our self-development, the challenge is to feel comfortable with the uncomfortable and behave predictably unpredictable. This of course will be frowned upon by many people, and for good reason (to them) ...because they will cease to control the fearless person who can meet that challenge.

———

One must never be overly concerned whether they are heading in the right or wrong direction, only that they are 'heading' and not stagnating.

Right and wrong are merely concepts relating to how people think today.

A person enjoying self-development will think very differently today compared to how they did in the past.

A stagnant person will think the same today as they did in the past.

———————

The beauty of life,
so gentle and calm,
its powerful strength,
to love and not harm.

Deep and connected sexual activity heightens the senses to such an extent that it will transcend a couple into a deep state of emotion. The connection must be loving, as anything less is a mistake. This can only occur between two people. Should more than two people be involved, it is vulgarity, and vulgarity can never be loving.

To fully connect and explore orgasmically is mind altering. First and foremost, it requires a truly loving connection and must be experienced with no thought of time. Hours will pass like minutes.

Emphasis will always be on pleasuring each other through feeling, never thought. The emphasis will never be placed on a 'must' basis, as with the right person, it will happen very naturally.

Allow feelings to guide, dispelling all thoughts. Thoughts only serve to distract and take away from the experience.

To really be in that moment with your partner, give way being totally open to one another's feelings.

Both people placing absolute subconscious focus on one another will result in an indescribable experience of connection.

Giving way to any inhibitions and really focusing externally is key to sexual enlightenment.

A couple can never experience this enlightenment if one, or both people are sexually inward focused, distracted, narrow minded, or in any kind of a hurry. If this is the case, the couple are not a good match.

The balance between love and lust is a precarious one. If balance is lost, frustration will follow.

Touch, not merely that of a physical nature but of mind and heart, is essential during deep and connected sexual experiences. If only the superficial physical nature of sexual pleasure is explored, then one can only ever experience sex on a superficial level. Of course, this can still bring much pleasure, but only of similar levels to that of any other activity one enjoys. To truly experience a sexual encounter with the most intense and indescribable feelings, one must give way completely to the moment, allowing all three elements: body, mind, and heart, to connect with that of another.

Only through experiences of such depth can humans wake up to life.

———————

There is little more attractive than a sense of humour.

Humour is such an important ingredient for happiness. Lack of laughter in the world is astounding. We take ourselves far too seriously at times and ought to realise how insignificant we are in terms of the planet and the universe. Once we accept this, we can stop our egos running wild, and intern end the easily offended and pathetic culture of the 'victim'. This odious populist culture only serves to undermine genuine victims in the world, i.e. those without food, shelter, or water, who experience horrific conditions.

Even in our darkest moments, it is so important to retain an insatiable sense of humour. No one has the right to take that away and indeed no one can, for it is us who must give in to another person/group's domination of us, allowing them to suppress the sense of humour we were born with.

'Laughter is the best medicine.'

Unfortunately, a sense of humour is often linked with a lack of seriousness, and so encouraged to be suppressed. This is very wrong. Happy people are all round more successful people. A sense of humour has no bearing whatsoever on a person's seriousness.

The richest person in the world is not necessarily the person with the most money, it is the happiest person.

Happiness and smiling go hand-in-hand. Love is associated with smiling. A sense of humour is associated with smiling. A sense of humour is extremely attractive. A smile is attractive. Laughter is attractive. Be an attractive person rather than a repulsive repellent.

Only a fool would choose to be miserable and heavy.

Laughter, humour, happiness, smiling, etc…are all extremely infectious characteristics that promote our wellbeing.

———

It is in our own best interest to live on a clean planet, free from pain, suffering, pollution, and threats of any kind. There really is no need for it.

The four necessities in life: food, water, shelter, love.

———————

Meditation is a very powerful and positive tool that no outside influence can affect.

To simply reconnect and allow freedom for the mind to journey wherever it pleases. To fully open with no influence whatsoever, to let go. To stop thinking. To feel.

One must cease to think, completely, if one is to meditate. Meditation cannot happen if the mind is full of clutter and nonsensical talk, or if any time restraint exists. One must carefully invest into the most precious commodity each of us has…ourselves.

———————

*The flâneur, with a carefree waltz and lightness of demeanour, sees
with their heart and hears with their soul.*

*The flâneur, with their casual grace and elegant procrastination,
they are no slave to conformity, and nothing ever takes its toll.*

*Life is their canvas, and they are their paint,
days filled with dreams, be them ever so quaint.*

*Observations in abundance, of the existence following their test,
with absent comprehension, that their ending is to be just like the
rest.*

*The flâneur, with their surreal ideal of romance, are destined to live
in perpetual pain, misunderstood and alone.*

*The flâneur, with their naive perception on the meaning of life, they
neither come nor go, and never feel at home.*

———————

We are conditioned by authority to work towards an asset-based life. What is that? The idea being that 'if it isn't tangible, it isn't worth it.' Is love tangible? How much money is enough? How many assets are enough? This is a superficial two-dimensional way to exist, which simply it is not living. People who follow this lifestyle are unintelligent and foolish humans who have missed the very essence of life.

It is difficult to imagine a person nearing their end in life and knowing so, wishing to spend their final moments alive with their material possessions or trying to earn more. It is far more likely that they would wish to be surrounded by loved ones. It is not a wild assumption to make to suggest that they would also likely feel some regret over not spending enough time with those loved ones.

It is very easy to be swallowed up by life, only to be hit later with deep regret once the realisation of priorities becomes apparent.

The way we lived yesterday matters no more. The way we live today, effects not only today, but tomorrow also.

One must never waste one moment of time living in regret.

———————

*Hardware (phone).   Software   (operating   system/apps).
Power (charge-electrical).*
*Hardware (human body).   Software (mind).
Power (love-heart).*

Without charge, a phone slowly runs out of power until it ceases to function.

Without love, a human follows the same pattern. We need love to charge us so that we too can function effectively.

A phone performs regular software updates to be effective and efficient.

A human must do the same or it becomes limited to its past way of thinking, eventually becoming incompatible with the evolving world and its people.

The physical phone itself must be well maintained otherwise it will not have much longevity.

The human body is no different, it must be well maintained in as broad a sense as possible.

Behind this analogous concept is love, the true power source of the human being.

———————

'Who would give a law to lovers? Love is unto itself a higher law.' - Boethius

What is marriage? What is a relationship? Why do humans feel the need to give ownership and take ownership of one another? Love is far deeper than taking ownership or controlling another.

An intimate relationship should never be the result of obligation or necessity. A successful intimate relationship is based first and foremost on love. An intimate relationship based on anything else, will ultimately lead to unhappiness.

To really love, is to feel an indescribable positive and powerful connection with another human. Real love has no rules, it is free to evolve and is in no way suffocating or claustrophobic.

Lovers will truly inspire, support and champion each other, unconditionally. They will not need each other, rather, they will want each other. They may not live in the same house, they may not even live in the same country, yet their mental connection remains perfectly intact. They have no insecurities with one another, they place no expectations or demands onto one another. They have no desire to possess one another. Voluntary loyalty goes hand in hand with love, demanded loyalty is a repellent of love.

———————

'Men are so simple and so much inclined to obey immediate needs that a deceiver will never lack victims for his deceptions.' - N. Machiavelli

We must fiercely resist and vehemently challenge others attempts to manipulate us using our age. For or a person who accepts another's opinions, will make decisions based on those opinions and lose control of their own life.

It is imperative that we continue to learn every day, maintaining and developing our youthful energy and enthusiasm to act. Knowledge combined with inaction is one of the greatest travesties of adulthood, leading to a decaying of the mind, body, and heart.

Regular exercise, sound nutrition, and adequate rest will increase a person's energy levels.

However, neither of those essential things will generate anywhere near the energy that a loving relationship will.

The key lies in love.

———————

When love is discovered, the mind, body and heart open freely with no boundaries, as though the correct combination has been uncovered on a Japanese puzzle box.

Life is very simple, yet we over complicate.

Love.

———————

Expectations are nothing but thoughts, they do not exist, they only serve to feed anxiety and disappointment.

To attain happiness, one must avoid the destructive path of expectation.

———

Procrastination is self-sabotaging behaviour responsible for killing dreams.

Excessive thought feeds the procrastinator who would rather cower away in their impotent comfort zone, rather than proactively ensure their own happiness.

The comfort zone is a very safe place to be but is tremendously detrimental to one's life. The scared person is the comfort zones biggest advocate.

Unfortunately, the procrastinator allows many great opportunities for happiness and love pass them by, often unnoticed.

———————

We place great emphasis on the concept of honesty. However, if one observes human reaction when honesty is spoken, it is rarely well received.

Society appears threatened by the truth.

'An honest man is always a child.' - Socrates

There is something refreshingly honest about young children. Although they on the cusp of letting their environment shape them to the point of extremely difficult return, they are honest, often brutally honest. They are also unashamedly corruptible.

This raises the question of the link between honesty and corruption, are they as linked as one may initially think?

To be 100% honest, requires great courage. Cowardice is the trait of dishonesty.

Corruptibility on the other hand is a much greyer area. Does the incorruptible human exist? Do we all have our 'price'?

We have a responsibility to ourselves to be honest. If we cannot be honest with ourselves, we cannot ever live in contentment.

Many people have developed such efficient mechanisms to deal with their self-deception that they convince themselves they are being honest. The feeling inside never lies.

———

Two of the most influential and unparalleled moments of clarity in a person's life:

1. The birth of their child.
2. The death of one or more of their immediate family.

Nothing will change the way one sees and approaches life with more impact.

The choice is simple, either allow that impact to be positive or negative.

The realisation of both the power and the fragility of life is very humbling.

———————

'Do you want to know who you are? Don't ask. Act! Action will delineate and define you.' – T. Jefferson

What is motivation? Where does it come from? What ignites it? What stifles it?

So many of us start out with dreams, dreams that take all shapes and sizes. Yet very few of us follow our dreams. Instead, we become swallowed up and spat out onto the conveyor belt of life. That is, we let external pressures and influenced derail our dreams.

This is very easily done. However, awareness combined with courage to act and say 'no', is a person's greatest ally in staying on-track and fuelling the motivational fire smouldering inside of us all, into a great roaring blaze.

The most powerful motivation in life, is love.

———

'The opinions and beliefs of men follow involuntarily the evidence proposed to their minds.' - T. Jefferson

This unfortunate truth is the path to mental and physical destruction.

'A sad soul can kill quicker than a germ.' - J. Steinbeck

———————

I feel like I am walking,
on a narrow wall 100ft high.
One side I live,
the other I die.

Without awareness,
things can be missed.
It's true that passion dies,
where love does not exist.

———————

To be in agonising emotional pain is a terribly paralysing feeling.

To trust another person with one's happiness, is a mistake perhaps bigger than any other.

Love should be avoided at all costs! It is a drain on our very existence.

We must learn to be alone in life and should another human spark feelings of warmth, it is imperative that those feelings be suppressed, or even better, quashed in an instant.

Be cold, be clinical and be driven to keep moving forward one step at a time. Never allowing ourselves to stand still for even the shortest of moments because if we do, life will get a firm grip and squeeze every last drop of energy from us.

This self-protective method is the path to contentment.

We must try to make as much money as we can, while we can.

Making money is more important than love.

Work is the main purpose of life.

To search for love is a foolish gamble simply not worth pursuing.

We must seek the approval of others.

Following is good for us.

Never ask difficult questions in case they cause offense.

What sort of human would desire the above existence? A fool? Yes, a fool.

'Some people die at 25 and aren't buried until 75.' - B. Franklin

We are natural explorers and to find ourselves, we must explore without limits, self-imposed or otherwise, in every direction imaginable inside and out of the mind, body and heart. This is the key to having a life and not merely an existence.

It is often said as motivation, that 'we only live once'.

A more accurate statement would be that 'we only die once'.

———————

Money dominates many people's existence. It drives them in a direction they would otherwise not be headed. As the donkey with the stick attached to its head with a water flask, slightly out of reach but very much in view. Make no mistake, it is nothing but a trick to get the most work out of the donkey, aka us.

Most people act in a subservient manner whenever money is involved. It truly can corrupt the mind, body, and heart if one does not understand that it does not exist, it is not real, it is only a 'man-made' concept with the sole aim to control. Unfortunately, it is a very successful invention that many humans are enslaved by.

Monetary gifts are often seen as a sign of affection. The idea being that, the more money spent somehow equals the more love given. This is a totally false premise.

Time is the most precious thing one human can give to another. Money is nothing more than a guilt easer for the fact one human has chosen not to give their time to another.

Money is not related to love in the slightest.

Time is directly related to love. The more one loves another, the more time they give to that person.

People that choose to be alone, are in-love with themselves.

It can be clearly seen how much interest one human has in another by the amount of distraction they allow to get in the way of giving their time.

It is unfortunate that money places so much temptation of greed onto weak humans who cannot resist its lure.

Financial gain at the expense of another is commonplace among people.

The true benefit of money is that it reveals the true character of a person.

———————

Selling education is a sickening idea and ought never to be tolerated.

Education is a human right.

———————

Why not try lots of things in life? Why not entertain lots of ideas and thoughts? Why try to convince ourselves that we, or they, are right.

What if we didn't follow anyone else's ideas about life, and instead dared to trust ourselves? Can we do this? Is this possible?

Can we cease to crave belonging to something or someone?

———————

As life becomes clearer and cleaner, one may find themself drifting
in and out of time.

———————

Love can be very strange at times. It can be very one sided, leaving a hurt and hollow feeling within.

It is not right to be a mere option to anybody. Such treatment is deplorable.

Those who are serious about love, love seriously.

Placing a loved one as a priority will never be a conscious decision. It will come purely subconsciously.

Anything other than love, effort is required, and so the priority is lost.

———————

To recalibrating the mind, all past influences must be disconnected from.

This sounds impossible when one first thinks about it. However, only through an awareness of influence, can one begin to really understand, with clarity, what it is to think and act for themselves.

It will be as though a thick fog has ascended, revealing a crystal clear and beautiful sight.

———————

'What strikes me is the fact that in our society, art has become something which is only related to objects, and not to individuals, or to life.' - M. Foucault

Humans fall very easily into the comfort trap, into a mundane, mechanical, and repetitive existence.

Our lives can very easily become nothing but repetition. Monotonous repetition. Repetition of actions and thoughts of those gone before.

To explore and do new things every single day is extremely important for us to not simply evolve, but evolve in happiness.

———————

Is the mind awake when the body is awake or asleep? Is the mind awake when the heart is found or lost?

The body must be maintained appropriately. Humans are often told about 'motivation', almost always by money-driven 'experts'. They push the belief through their clever marketing and manipulation that we must be in state-of-the-art gymnasiums or somehow, we are letting ourselves down. This is utter nonsense!

We do not need to be in some special place in order to develop our bodies. We do not have to pay money to any business or person to develop ourselves.

These 'experts' will try every way possible to take money from people, using all the buzzwords they learned while 'studying' to manipulate.

We do not need anyone to tell us how to do what we have been doing since the beginning of humanity, that is, simply to move regularly.

To engage with the body, we do not require any fanciful gymnasiums with all the sparkly tempting equipment. We only require an open mind free of limitation.

———

Teachers serve their purpose, but they must never be followed.

A true teacher encourages their student to think and act independently of themselves.

Because a person knows how to use cutlery, does not make them a chef.

It is the failing of many 'teachers' in life to believe they know it all. Or that they can only learn from those of higher 'standing'.

A wise person knows how little they know. We are all teachers and learners, regardless of age, social or academic background, yet there is a certain arrogance about humans around that mid-life period. They often radiate an air of superiority over the young and old, as though their time and 'knowledge' is so important and correct. Thinking such a way is wrong.

What does it mean to be 'educated'? Many would perhaps surmise that to mean academically. And that is true in part, but there are many forms of 'education'.

———————

Exploring what really matters in life…if all else were gone, if we found ourselves stranded on a desert island, alone, what would be the essentials that we would desire?

It is not an unreasonable assumption to suggestion that one would miss the feeling of human interaction, connection, and love.

It is inconceivable to think that a human would miss money and/or status.

What are the essentials in life? Food, water, shelter, and love.

So many people miss the obvious essence of life. Love. How is this possible? Why do we go through life giving little to no priority to this essence?

If people can truly wake up to reality and what truly and obviously matters, they will then develop and progress in ways never seen before.

———————

To live my life,
through eyes that not only look, but really see.
To smile inexplicably,
at the most perfect person, who smiles back at me.

Being true to myself,
accepting how I feel.
Allowing my heart to be my compass,
I will wake someplace real.

———

Many humans agonise over being where they were at some point in the past, or where the want to be in the future, or where they thought in the past that they would be today.

Happiness lies in simply being, today.

How can anyone truly be alive if they are focused on what has been and what may never be?

The past nor future exist, only now, right now, this very second, this is what exists.

———————

'Good' and 'bad' are subjective, anyone can build someone else up or bring them down by telling them they are good or bad. It only holds meaning if sanction is given.

If a child or spouse is scolded repeatedly, they will behave in one of two ways, either they will respond in a similar way, with aggressive conflict or they will cower away. Either way, actions have impacted and shaped their actions and subsequent actions.

With knowledge and understanding of this, why would humans not encourage and show great love and respect to other humans? This is how we develop and live in happiness.

Why form any negative thoughts? Why? Why direct any negativity towards another human being? If we can understand the seemingly obvious fact that our own actions or even inactions, be them verbal or physical, shape the world that we live in, then we will start to really understand that we really do create the world we live in.

What does this say about us as a species, based on the world we live, today? Intelligent?

Uncovering the origins of our thoughts and feelings is of great importance.

———————

Religion, money, patriotism, ignorance, tribalism...all fuel conflict.

Anyone with intelligence would not choose to be part of these things.

The reality is that many do not choose to be part of them. Unfortunately, most parents indoctrinate their children from birth, leaving them little to no hope of becoming an individual thinking.

Parents are responsible for the world we live in.

———————

To reach the apex of life and stay there, one must be totally free of all external influence and environmental shaping. Being 100% honest and truthful with oneself in the present.

———————

'Beware of those who are bored and not passionate about life, for they will bore you with reasons for not living.' – S. Kassem

'Love' is a word that is thrown around so easily. Often said with as much effort as it takes to blink the eyes.

Love is not 'love', it cannot be defined by a simple word. If one thinks it can, they do not understand love.

Love is not ownership, lust, sex, companionship, judgment, jealousy, suffocating, cold, dominating, negativity, game playing, or any of that nonsense. There are no obligations with love. Love is not marriage, it is not simply living together, wearing a ring on a certain finger, or saying a few words in front of a collective audience. It is never forced and never hurts.

Rather, love is very gentle, it is nourishing, warm, beautiful, magnetic, contentment, priority, and purity. It is losing all concept of time and distraction. It is an extraordinary feeling of happiness, of safety. Love is the true meaning of life.

Whether love is believed or not, it makes no difference, the world will still turn, and people will still go about their routine day after day until they die. But to let a person know they are loved, to trust that person enough to completely open yourself up 100%, knowing that person could destroy you mentally. To give that person full access and be willing to trust them to be the only person in the world to know everything about you, and in the same light want to know everything about them. To get lost with that person every time in their presence.

Would that not be a nice way to live life? To live fully and honestly?

Surely it is obvious that if we are dishonest, we are mere cowards? It is easy to lie and to live a lie, that takes no virtue at all. But to be honest with ourselves and the person we love, and live the only life we get, truly, this cannot be a wasted life.

———————

'Love' is a word so often used,
Misunderstood by many.
Diluted, polluted and meaningless.

Love is so much more than a word,
The value of which is found in action.
Baring the sweetest feelings of warmth.

Love is weightless and free,
It has no rules or expectations.
Love is the person we see so clearly within.

———

'It isn't what we say or think that defines us, but what we do.' – J. Austen

As time moves on, negative personality habits can become more engrained and therefore more difficult to change, but not impossible.

Moving to a new environment and forming new positive habits is essential to the changing process. However, one must be very careful not to find themselves 'out of the frying pan into the fire' i.e. from a bad situation to one that maybe different but equally as harmful, if not worse.

Change will only bring positivity if it is positive change. Change that brings unsurpassed energy, and happiness.

Fear must never stifle much needed and wanted change.

Change is never a straight path, it is more zig zagging in the right direction.

Never be deterred if the first attempt at change is unsuccessful. It is all data gathering.

To make mistakes is not bad, to repeat mistakes is bad.

It is impossible to change by repeating the same cycles over and over.

Reinventing oneself is a mechanism that all humans possess.

Unfortunately, not all humans wishing to change, have the courage to do so.

Again, the culprit is fear.

———

Discovering the unique person who one can reciprocally be
completely open and honest with, is extremely rare.

Freedom to live can only be achieved through honesty to oneself.

———————

To hand power of oneself to another human is incredibly weak and shows great insecurity.

To believe someone else can direct one's life is absurd, and nothing more than an actor being directed by a movie director. An actor maybe good and a director maybe equally as good, perhaps even more talented, but it will only ever be the director's vision that the actor is performing. And actually, the director is almost always working to someone else's story.

Why would any human wish to live their live guided by another human, based on their vision? This is to live as nothing more than an extension of another human. It is a waste of life and only serves to fuel egotistical humans who crave dominant control.

To live a life following the direction, guidance, and approval of another is fake no matter how it may be cleverly disguised.

Good actors can be very convincing that they are not acting, that goes the same for weak minded people who seek approval of others. They cannot admit to themselves that they are living their life literally being told what to do by another.

One cannot go wrong if they trust themselves, being 100% honest in the mirror.

This inner harmony is incredibly powerful and will project itself outward, inspiring others.

To inspire is positive, to control is negative.

Controlling people are very common and unfortunately mistaken for inspirational people, of whom are very rare.

Controlling people have many faces and are adept in manipulation.

Nobody likes to think of themselves as being controlled, manipulated, or dominated. However, it does not stop the unfortunate reality being true.

———

One cannot truly be free,
whose mind does not clearly see.

For as darkness fills a deep hole,
living a lie will subdue the soul.

Do it with passion, or do not do it at all.

———————

The feeling of being lost comes from a resistance to the truth within.

We know the answers to our 'problems', but very few have the courage to honestly admit those answers due to paralysis caused by fear.

'Over analysis leads to paralysis.'

All humans experience fear at some point, but they must never allow fear to affect their choices, dominate or control them.

Clear choices made with or without fear are very important in establishing one's inner strength.

Failing to make difficult choices due to fear, will result in a snowballing effect of weakness within. Two things will follow this behaviour:

      1. A person will stagnate.
      2. A person will hand control of their live to another person/group.

Making obvious and sometimes very difficult choices will result in a real individual life of unimaginably happiness. Fail to make those choices and live an unhappy lie.

If one is honest with themself, they can seldom go wrong.

———

The meaning of life is not complicated, it requires no education or money, it is very simply, love.

Love it is shrouded in materialistic nonsense and grand gestures.

Love cannot be marketed and/or used like an object.

Love is untouchable, yet it can be felt with such power.

To understand love, one must let go and never try to control it. The very second a person tries to control or harness love, it ceases to exist.

Love is unconditional.

Unconditionally, many people base their life around conditions, conditioning, control, etc. They do things, more often than not, under condition. Very seldom does a person simply act without thought of what they may receive in return, or what may happen if they do or do not act.

To act without thought would mean to act without fear, it would mean to act honestly and purely.

If humans act without thought, completely without thought, they will always be guided from within towards love.

We are not born to hate, lie, cheat, thieve, and all that negative nonsense. We are born to love, and with love, naturally comes laughter, warmth, and affection.

Only when humans overthink, do the problems begin.

Let go of thought and let love take over.

———————

Technology is a very good way of determining whether a human is interested in another human.

To be completely attentive to a person, not forced or demanded, to share a moment of complete intimacy, physically or mentally, or both, is to know love.

———————

It is very easy to judge another.

It is extremely difficult to know someone and see them with fresh eyes, with not one ounce of judgement.

Is an active human better than a reactive human?

Reactive humans are fearful and merely exist.

Active humans are driven in pursuit of pleasure.

Is it possible to be neither, or both, without though?

Can humans just be, without consciously acting or reacting, just be?

So much conflict exists through action and reaction.

What if we could see with our senses, without thought and without guidance from someone else's senses?

It is so important for us to see clearly and honestly, the balance of life and how important it is the let go and allow ourselves to come to this balance naturally, neither consciously nor subconsciously, just completely open and naturally, without any resistance.

———————

The untrained mind is murky and can never see clearly.

The question is, how do we train the mind?

The beginning of this training happens the moment we trust our very own instincts and dispel from within, all traces of indoctrination.

Unless we are healthy and free in mind, then we are nothing more than someone else's slave.

It appears so much easier to be honest with others than it is to be honest with ourselves.

We must never allow fear of the truth to control the way we think and feel.

No other person has any right to tell us how to feel and think.

We get one attempt at life, it's our choice whether or not we give ownership of that life to someone else, or to a group of people and their ideas.

No one can be original and free if they follow.

Would anyone really volunteer themselves into slavery?

To unwittingly, or even worse, wittingly volunteer oneself to another's ideals, is a waste of life.

Self-empowerment comes to those who train their minds to be free and honest.

____

Our system pushes us constantly to produce. If we are not productive
then we are perceived as bad.

Most people feel obligated to be productive. For whose benefit?

The more productive we are, the most successful it is perceived we
are.

Question this notion.

———————

It is unfair to use physical strength to dominate and get ahead, but it is acceptable to use mental strength.

Yet intelligent people used their mental strength to dominate the physically strong, and the physically strong do not realise this because they are not so intelligent.

To dedicate oneself to physical or mental training will surely determine the field as to where a person's strength lies. Can a person dedicate themselves to both areas and be an expert in both?

Of course, lots of people exist who have a good level of both mental and physical ability and skill, but the real experts and specialists show clear characteristics of where their expertise lie.

Is it okay for a physically strong person to use that strength to take what they feel they are entitled too? Many would say 'no'. Yet it seems quite acceptable for a mentally stronger human to succeed by using their dominant skill to 'get ahead' and take what they feel they are entitled too. Often by manipulating and subduing the physically stronger. Brains vs Brawn.

The Darwinian theory of 'survival of the fittest' has merely been replaced with 'survival of the intelligent'.

———————

'the greater the outward show, the greater the inward poverty' - J. krishnamurti

Be authentic.

———————

One can only change the future, from today.

———————

Sensitivity is a rare and precious trait.

People have become so hardened to the world. This hardening is infectious and spreads very quickly among people.

To be sensitive is not a weakness, it is a strength, a powerful and positive strength.

Can we truly love if we are cold and hardened people devoid of emotion?

Is it a sign of strength to be insensitive?

A fine line exists between education, miseducation, and indoctrination. One must be very careful not the fall victim of the latter two, for they will contaminate the mind.

Is it possible to think pure uncontaminated thoughts?

Thinking, is not a negative activity by any means. However, contaminated thinking is absolutely a negative activity.

It is often the engrained contaminated thinking, that drives the subconscious contaminated thought.
Education is essential for humans to evolve, of course. However, it must be questioned and challenged constantly for it to develop honestly.

One can never be overeducated. However, one can certainly become miseducated and indoctrinated.

Is that difficult to see? Or, difficult to admit? Pride?

One who can admit they have made a mistake, no matter what that mistake, takes the biggest leap into the correct and true area of life.

It is often said that it takes courage to admit when one is wrong, this is yet more self-limiting nonsense that humans have put in their own way. It is not difficult, nor does it take courage to admit when one has made a mistake. It is the easiest of things to do and will have the most advantageous outcome and positive impact to one's life.

———————

The limits to our mental capabilities are unbelievably misunderstood.

We can see so clearly our physical capabilities and what we can achieve, one only need observe various athletes and the margins to which they are breaking physical records, but we are merely scratching the surface of our mental capabilities.

Our mental capabilities must be allowed freedom to explore, in order to flourish, develop and perform beyond our current comprehension.

It is incredibly easy to allow ourselves to become enslaved and entangled in self-made complex systems that are not real.

The reason can be traced directly back to miseducation and indoctrination.

These two powerful enemies of human beings must be completely eradicated if we are to succeed long term as happy and healthy people.

Observing with honest eyes the self-limiting systems that we blindly follow, will allow us an appreciation of how unnecessarily complex we have made our existence.

Failure to recognise this will result in us living in nothing more than an image of life that we will never arrive at.

———————

With all the complexities and noise around us, is it possible to really understand? Or do we simply understand what we are told to understand?

Many egotists like to pontificate and subdue with plentiful advice, backed up with their apparent vast array of impressive 'knowledge', but do they understand anything more than how to control.

Is being able to control, a desired ability?

Would anyone wish to be controlled or to control? Surely it would be better not to control or be controlled? Surely it would be better to treat each other with respect and care, with no hidden agenda based around control?

It is easy for on to see that control exists everywhere.

Can we find understanding from within? Is this possible?

When a child is born, does it not have an inner guide that drives it to frown and cry when unhappy, smile and laugh when happy? No 'expert' need teach them to do so, it is completely innate, naturally coming from within.

And so, can a person tell another how to love? Is love not that same natural innate occurrence?

Specialist analysts would of course no doubt be able to write books on the subject, giving impressive talks to the willing masses. But what can they really tell people about the beauty that lies within a new-born baby or in a human that is feeling love deep inside of them?

Love exists without any need for discussion, it is there for all to see, all anybody need do is open their heart and feel.

This simplicity cuts right through life and no so-called 'experts' are necessary for proof of loves existence.

One must never allow another person or thing to spoil their senses.

———————

No one can monopolise 'understanding'.

Once an awareness of understanding exists, real power exists.

Understanding will cause many unwelcome effects in certain people one surrounds themself with.

It is important to keep in mind that people who are not of true and honest character, are not worth a second thought.

Those of pure innocence and sincerity (often unwittingly), will welcome and reinforce such radical change in others, even if they do not understand the cause or effect of the change.

Such people are very rare and ought to be highly valued and respected.

Only a self-righteous self-centres jealous idiot would negatively knock a person because they are trying to better themself.

———————

Most people are addicted to the very routine that causes them unhappiness.

———————

What is wisdom? Who is 'wise'? Is it wise to love, or resist love?

To have a love of wisdom, one must first understand love, otherwise there can be no real wisdom, only a theory of what it is to be wise.

Does wisdom exist today, or has it been swallowed up by the lust for imperium?

As is almost always the case, the shallow and manipulative trait that exists in all humans, rears its ugly head, driving people to control and 'organise' the pure and honest intentions of the human being.

Power-driven humans see opportunity to control and they seize it, forming cleverly structured groups, organisations, and cults, using the past as their focal point to prey on the weak minds of today. It is not so difficult to see past the unsophisticated rhetoric if one simply opens their eyes, ears, mind, and heart.

True wisdom has no teacher, no rigid structure or organisation. One cannot claim to be wise, or a teacher of wisdom. And if such a person or organisation does, this should raise many questions as to the authenticity of the source.

Name dropping and worshipping so called past-masters, temples, or whatever other nonsense, is at very best, history, but it is not related to wisdom. Quite the opposite.

The hierarchical dominance underpinning this type of ideology, is nothing more than manipulative mind control. It is certainly not enlightenment, it is endarkenment. Mere domination and submission.

True wisdom cannot be harnessed, packaged, marketed, bought, or sold. True wisdom is open and free, it is not tangible, not arrogant, nor full of hubris. True wisdom is empowering, inspiring, and full of love and meaning. There is no striving for 'more', for example, MORE beauty, MORE love, MORE knowledge, etc, there simply 'is'. There IS beauty, there IS love and there IS knowledge, these things exist, they are. Only when one grasps and really sees with clarity this fact, can they understand the magnitude and destructiveness of these phoney images on the cave wall, and the reality that the cave itself is nothing more than a big manipulative lie.

'Comrades! We must abolish the cult of the individual once and for all.' – N. Khrushchev

Love exists inside all human beings.

Not all human beings can love.

———————

Can we be completely honest with ourselves?

We are often very passionate about and place great value on being honest with others, but what about the passion and value we place on being honest with ourselves?

If we cannot be true to ourselves, our lives are simply built on lies.

From lies, comes conflict and unhappiness.

Is it not better to value ourselves? Is that not a good idea?

If a person does not value themself, can they truly value others?

Can they truly value life?

The person who values every second of life, is intelligent.

———————

Making money is not difficult.

It is what one is prepared to sacrifice in order to make money that sets those with money apart from those without money.

Humans have created a world whereby those with money are celebrated and looked upon as role models.

People aspire to be like the financially wealthy.

Money is a very good indicator of a person's true character.

How much money does one need?

Is it not obscene that millionaires and billionaires exist in a world where humans die of starvation, where humans are going blind because they do not have, for example, simple eye drops to counteract conjunctivitis, eye drops that in some countries are free?

How can people who accrue disgusting amounts of financial wealth be so admired?

How can these people look in the mirror, knowing that people are dying of hunger, little children dying of hunger? It seems so wrong, and clearly shows how very mixed up human priorities are.

Surely these people ought to be looked at as feckless rather than revered?

The equal distribution of common decency around the globe, is surely a better idea to strive for than simply to make money?

———————

When two people meet in life and the connection is greater than anything either has experienced before, when there is an indescribable 'pull' towards each other, when the only negative part of them being together is when they leave each other, is that love?

Is it love to be unconditionally drawn to someone? To enjoy simply being in their presence? No agenda, no judgment, no expectations, no negativity, no uncomfortable silences, nothing but the warmest and content feelings within, is this love?

'I love this song', 'I love this food', 'I love…', is any of that really love?

Love is not all dissimilar to an iceberg, in that the tip of the iceberg is the 'love' part, but love has great underlying solid foundations of which it is built.

Love is underpinned by such things as trust, loyalty, happiness, support, priority, etc, all of which unconditional.

Love is indefinable. It is a power way beyond human understanding. Yet, many try to understand and think about love.

Many try to control, sell, buy, manipulate, nurture, and expand love. But love cannot be controlled or thought about, love simply is, it exists.

If a human is fortunate enough to connect in depths of inexplicable feelings of 'love', it is silly, given how short we as humans exist in our life cycle, not to allow that love to exist in harmony.

Balance is a beautiful thing and not to be underestimated. With love comes only good.

However, it is unfortunate that humans often allow themselves to be guided by those who do not have love in their life.

Be aware of humans who offer negative advice on love, this is a clear indication that they themselves have never felt love. This is of course unfortunate for them, but it cannot be stressed enough that it is their problem, and they have no right to be offering advice on something they know nothing about.

Danger exists when a human in a position of authority freely offers advice to those who look to them for guidance, on such matters they have no experience in.

A true mentor knows what to say and perhaps more importantly, what not to say to their students, family, friends, etc… It is very dangerous to assume that because someone is an 'expert' in their chosen field, that it somehow qualifies them to offer advice or be an authority in other fields.

The world is a small place and humans are even smaller.

Our significance and importance are grossly overestimated by ourselves.

———

"The ruling class in every age have tried to impose a false view of the world upon their followers." – G. Orwell

———————

Are perspectives and priorities as important as social acceptance? What would the world look like if no human lied? Would we be happier? Do we lie in order to be socially accepted? What is social acceptance? Is it necessary? I want to belong and be accepted by this group of people, so I will lie to myself so that I am accepted. Is that a good way to live? What if all the people in the group feel the same? The entire group is then a complete lie. Who would want to be part of such a group?

Yet humans do this, almost every day. Lying repeatedly to others and themselves, simply to be accepted, to 'fit in'. It is a union mentality, 'we are safer in numbers'? Safer from who? From the other groups built on lies? Why not tell the truth? True freedom comes when the truth is told.

Every lie is like erecting a vertical bar. Many lies means many bars. Before long, one is imprisoned by their own lies. To stop lying is very easy to do and will bring immense freedom to life.

Lies bring nothing but hurt.

A successful liar (oxymoron) may convince others and indeed make them happy, but inside, the liar is not happy and is always filled with pain.

Lies become so natural and so complex, that liars will often believe that they are 'too far gone' to change. This is nonsense, everybody can change in an instant.

Truth is incredibly important.

It is the test of one's character to be truthful.

———————

A good teacher will teach how to wield the tools of life. Though they will not teach what type of life to build.

A chef ought to teach their apprentice all the techniques within the kitchen. But if they then teach their student to remake their own signature dish repeatedly, then how can their apprentice ever be free to explore their own recipes and build their own repertoire?

This method of teaching only serves to create robotic societies, fearful of independence and fearful of exploring their own potential.

———

Parenting is simple but requires strength of character.

Not all humans possess the strength of character to parent successfully.

At the birth of a child, a parent should be 100% the parent.
As the child develops, the parent becomes 90% parent/10% best friend.
By teens, 10% parent/90% best friend.
By adulthood, 1% parent/99% best friend.

The necessity of parenting cannot be overstated.

Weak people choose not to parent, taking the easier option of being their child's friend.

Pathetic people neither parent nor are their child's best friend.

A successful parent will produce an independent human, full of love and kindness, healthy and strong, mentally, and physically, with full control over fear, competitive only with themselves, open minded, full of positivity and fresh ideas.

An unsuccessful parent will produce a dependent human, cold when it comes to love and kindness, mentally and/or physically weak, with little to no control over fear, competitive only with others, narrow minded, full of negativity and excuses.

———

Educate to inspire and improve, never educate to control.

Be vigilant of those educating to control, as these loathsome manipulators unfortunately exist in abundance.

————

If we died today, the world would still turn. Maintaining awareness of this fact is essential in understanding the priorities of love and happiness.

The work we do, that we are convinced is so important...isn't.

Finances we stress over...why?

The trivial arguments...meaningless!

Why follow a monotonous life of suffering and struggle when one day, we will die...FACT! And likely that very same day, we will be replaced in some way, for example, at work.

Can the same be said relating to love? If a person we love died today, could we replace them the very same day? No. Why? Because the difference between love and work is incomparable.

Love should be given the upmost importance; work is merely a means to an end.

Work obsessed people are empty people.

This is not always clear for people who fall victim to this pattern, to see. It is the result of an insufficient upbringing lacking in love.

These types of people are extremely sad to see, especially when one holds love towards them.

Often dogmatic people, these people should be used as an example of how not to live happily.

All the post-nominal letters, titles and money cannot replace a love.

Sharing a bed with the right person, hearing them breath as they sleep, noticing every little detail, being close, laughing together, the way they look at you across a busy room, the way they always put you before anything or anyone else, the way distractions always come second to them, knowing without doubt that you are their priority, etc…this is truly beautiful.

To be too busy for love is one of the saddest and most foolish things to see one do.

———————

"He who regards himself only, and enters upon friendships for this reason, reckons wrongly... These are the so-called "fair-weather" friendships; one who is chosen for the sake of utility will be satisfactory only so long as he is useful... He who begins to be your friend because it pays will also cease because it pays." - Seneca

Many humans like to organise in groups. Groups that offer privileges to make its members to feel special.

Why would any sane person willingly join a hierarchy that purely exists because another human once decided it should? This is very unintelligent and not in any way conducive to happiness.

Why do certain humans like to group themselves? Why do they like to use secrecy as a bond? Is it a test of loyalty? Does keeping a secret from another mean a person is trustworthy?

If one chooses not to be part of a group, does that negate their worth? Negate their knowledge? Negate their ability to learn?

Does it mean they are not as valuable as those who choose to be part of groups?

Are groups mere magnets for people with low self-esteem? Or, do groups target those with low self-esteem? People with low self-esteem enjoy groups as it gives them a sense (albeit false) of importance.

Where there are groups of people who operate in secrecy and promote division and fear transparency, there will always be unhappy people...both inside and outside of the group.

Are groups necessary?

Cliques of lonely people.

Does the absence of love make for a success life?

What is a life without love? Is it not empty?

———————

'The same people who sell the panic, sell the pill' - Unknown.

Manipulation 101...

> 1. Convince people a problem exists.
> 2. Convince them you hold the solution.

It does not take much intelligence to see this everywhere.

———

Today, many experts exist, yet very few know how to live.

What is the point of knowledge if one is not knowledgeable on how to be happy? This is not intelligence, that is pure unintelligence.

Most people are too busy chasing other people's ideas of success, to notice what really matters.

When are we at our happiest? Surely it is with the ones we love? Surely it is when our hearts are beating with butterflies because we have the most intense loving feelings induced by another person? Surely it is when we are sharing moments of joy and warmth with another person? Surely it isn't chasing something deemed important by others?

———

Is it wise to live life around other people's negative experiences to the detriment of one's own positive experience?

One should never look to others experiences to guide their own when they know inside themselves what is right.

People with low self-esteem trust others about their own life. It is incredibly weak.

If actions must influence, one must allow their own actions influence others, never the other way around.

Influence people to wake up and start their own engines, but never influence them on what direction to go. Encourage them to make their own choices with conviction and courage.

———————

"When, therefore, we maintain that pleasure is the end, we do not mean the pleasures of profligates and those that consist in sensuality, as is supposed by some who are either ignorant or disagree with us or do not understand, but freedom from pain in the body and from trouble in the mind. For it is not continuous drinkings and revelings, nor the satisfaction of lusts, nor the enjoyment of fish and other luxuries of the wealthy table, which produce a pleasant life, but sober reasoning, searching out the motives for all choice and avoidance, and banishing mere opinions, to which are due the greatest disturbance of the spirit." - Epicurus

Love.

———————————

Polygamy cannot exist alongside real love. The moment a human entertains the idea inside their mind of an open or additional relationship, they have confirmed that no love exists with their current partner.

Polygamy can of course exist in sex-only based relationships, but never in relationship formed with love.

Sex-only based relationships are damaging, degrading, and devaluing to humans.

To seek sexual pleasure via different partners is no different to that of a human who uses drugs for pleasure, both have psychological problems and will never fill the void that exists inside of them.

Is life about accruing as much financial wealth as possible and then dying?

Is it about monotony?

Is it about a piece of land, a religion, or a possession?

Is it about enjoyment?

Is it about happiness?

Is it about love?

———————

So busy.

So many 'friends'.

Yet still so lonely.

The unfortunate and unnecessary reality of many who do not prioritise love.

Is what a person does not know, more important than what they do know?

Many people acquire knowledge to the cost of irreplaceable time that could have been better spent.

People who make this choice are very foolish.

Listening is an art that one must study with care.

People who constantly preach are incapable of truly listening as they are selfish and arrogant people. However, they are not foolish and gullible like their audience.

With no problems of low self-esteem themselves, preachers rely on weak minded people with low self-esteem.

It is common for people to portray an appearance of interest. However, most are busy formulating their own thing to say while others speak. This is not listening, it is nothing but disrespectful, arrogant, and rude.

Many people listen with no critical thought, they absorb almost 100% of what they are told, this is a low self-esteem and intelligence issue.

Some people listen completely, with critical thought. They will enquire and get to the root of the discussion, challenging areas of weakness, never simply accepting what they are told. This is listening. This is how the truth is arrived at. This is how humans develop.

If an idea can be challenged for all its weaknesses and apparent strengths, and still stand strong, this is an idea worth enquiring into further. That does not mean necessary believing in.
Weak ideas that are preached with no welcomed critical analysis, ideas that are told in a manner of which they must be accepted without question, are ideas that must always be walked away from in an instant.

There is an obvious reason that certain people/groups do not like questions…they are power hungry manipulators, and their followers are weak, gullible, and lonely.

Never follow.

To explore with a horizontally mindset that we are doing so side by side is very beneficial. But to follow with a vertical hierarchical mindset, looking up and down at people, is a waste of life.

———————

Attractive and/or successful people can have money.

But money itself does not make a person attractive and/or successful.

If a person is deemed attractive and/or successful simply because they have money, then the eyes reaching this conclusion are extremely poor, and their heart itself is ugly.

Not all wealthy people are successful, but all successful people have love.

———————

To think negatively or positively, is an option that we choose, ourselves.

Negative thinking creates selfish, 'doom and gloom', resentful, inward-focused, cold, unpleasant, unhealthy, and boring people.

Positive thinking creates altruistic, happy, healthy, loving, outgoing, joyful, and fun people.

Be careful not to be drawn in by negative thinkers, they are energy sappers.

———————

'As long as you are alive, you will either live to accomplish your own goals and dreams or be used to accomplish someone else's' – G. Cardone

Work is work no matter how it is disguised.

Work can give purpose; however, true purpose lies in love.

The 'wake-up + work + home + dinner + screen-time + sleep' routine, with the weekends and a few weeks a year holiday, gives purpose to who? The owners of the companies/institutions one works for? The governments who see its people as nothing more than commodities?

Who in their sane mind chooses such a slavish and manipulated existence?

———

A natural indicator of love is priority.

Never forced or requiring effort, those in-love will always find a way to communicate physically and mentally with each other, no matter what the circumstances.

To unconditionally prioritise a person is one of the highest levels of love.

It is the small things that make up the elements of love, not the grand gestures.

It is easy to do the grand gestures, they require little thought.

It is the small thoughtful things that truly reflect a person's seriousness and attentiveness towards another.

———————

A spoken word in the ear of someone who is listening can hold so much power, control, and influence.

One must always remain vigilant of whose words they allow to penetrate.

Never do people with bad intentions come with an obvious sign, unfortunately. Rather, they are often extremely clever and manipulative people who wear a cloak of trust.

The most adept of these odious people will often sow seeds of doubt into the minds of their victims, against those they see as a threat to their control.

Only those intelligently awake can see right through this fake cloak.

———————

Effort investment is directly linked to success.

Is it a surprise that those who are content in love, invest more quality time and effort into each other?

Is it a surprise that those content in love are very happy?

Those smart enough to invest in love, will reap happiness. Very simply put, those who don't, won't.

———————

It is easy to lose oneself.

If one is to find themself, they must never succumb to religious or non-religious dogma. This leads simply to a life of struggle and survival.

Pride will keep many people locked into their dogmatic behaviour. Courage will set them free.

Religious and non-religious organisations operate very similarly to the moth and the flame/light bulb. The moth can only see the light bulb it keeps banging into, burning itself until it dies. Blinded by the light, it cannot seem to see that there is life beyond. That the light it believes to be good, that it sees so clearly, does not care for it, and does not love it. The light feels nothing for the moth, yet the moth devotes its time and energy, ultimately laying down its life for the light.

When does the light attract the moth? During darkness, when the moth cannot see properly, when it is vulnerable and looking for light.

It is difficult to discuss love in terms of believing or not believing in it. That would be the equivalent of questioning the existence of the senses.

If the question were asked 'do you believe in the sense of smell?', it would seem silly. Love is a sense, just as vision, hearing, smell, touch, and taste.

It is important for people to trust themselves and not seek advice from others on the sense of love.

Would a sane person base their own food tastes on another's?

Would a songwriter be wise to trust the opinion of a deaf person? Would a painter be wise to ask the opinion of a blind person? How can one be sure they are not taking advice on love, from a person with little to no sense of love, with no heart?

Be authentic in love.

'No one is you and that is your power.' - D. Grohl

———————

Control is based around possession and power. It is the ability to manage and manipulate another human(s) into acting and thinking the way one commands.

Control can be indirect, direct, or both.

Reinforcement, both positive and negative, is crucial to the success of a controller.

What kind of person would want to control another? What kind of person would want to be controlled by another?

To control, or want to control another human, is a sign of great insecurity, not power.

To be controlled, or want to be controlled by another human, is also a sign of great insecurity, not trust.

These two types of people rely on each other to feed each other's insecurities. It is simple domination and submission.

Historical and modern culture glorifies both types of control-based behaviours, making them appear desirable.

This behaviour is as addictive and beneficial as drugs. It has no positive worth at all. As the drug dealer depends on the drug user, the controller depends on the controlled. They each fulfil the others wants and needs, depending on each other, never in a healthy way. Neither one could exist without the other. Supply and demand.

Like the beaten dog (controlled) who cowers down to its abusive owner (controller). The bad owner depends on the dog as much as the dog depends on its owner. But if that dog is taken out of that environment, the only environment it has ever known, and placed into a positive environment, the dog will in-time, flourish. The owner, however, will remain very frustrated until it finds another 'thing' to control.

It is very difficult for both the controller and the controlled to see and understand their behaviour, as both characters share the traits of denial and more ironically...pride.

This type of relationship manifests itself in many forms, home, work life, friends, family, etc.

The idea of 'the boss' is central to that of dominance. It is very simple, if one thinks of them self as a boss, they are the controller, the dominant person, the abuser. If one thinks of them self as having a boss, they are the controlled, the submissive person, the victim.

Control is restrictive and limiting to human potential, and nothing more than abuse.

Unfortunately, it is not always so clear to see when one has become the abuser or the victim.

Control kills dreams.

Control thrives on obedience.

To know you are a controller...ask the very simple question:
1. Am I telling anyone what to do, in any way, no matter how small or whatever the apparent justification?

To know you are controlled...ask the very simple questions:
1. Am I doing as I am told to do, in any way, no matter how small or whatever the apparent justification?

A very dangerous person is the person who has to ability to control many.

To free oneself of control, be it either the controller or the controlled, is incredibly empowering.

Is it such a problem to accept the model of the controller and the controlled if they are both content?

The problem arises when a person external to the controlled, but linked to them, becomes aware of a controlling situation. Such a person, usually a friend, naturally feels the need to 'help' the controlled 'break free' from the controller. But why? Why intervene at all? One such theory could be that as humans, our sense of justice is against all forms of slavery, and that at the route of slavery is control.

If a human sees another enslaved by someone or some group, it is only natural to want to free that person? To liberate them, allowing them to grow and experience life in their own way, free of control.

When the external person tries to free the controlled person from the controlling person, they are usually met with resistance. Stockholm Syndrome is very common in this situation. The situation can be made worse when the controlled confides in the controller about the external person. The controller then very shrewdly uses yet more manipulation on the controlled to convince them into believing the external person is the real controller. This then reinforces the controlled person's commitment to the controller, making the situation even worse.

In this situation, the external friend is usually pushed away and 'cut off'.

Time always reveals the truth to the controlled person.

The unfortunate thing, however, is that we cannot get time back. The controller has stolen precious time that the controlled person can never retrieve.

The controlled person should never feel unable to contact the external friend.

A true friend is always a friend.

———————

If we were trees, and the people we met were roots or leaves…hold on to the roots, as the leaves will come and go depending on the weather.

Roots are supportive and securing.

Leaves are happy while the sun is shining, but when the storm hits and the temperature drops, they disappear.

———————

Jealousy is a very powerful emotion of insecurity that originates from fear.

Fear originates from upbringing.

There is tremendous irony in love related jealousy.

This type of jealousy is an emotional response caused through fear of losing the very person one is likely to lose by allowing jealousy to direct their behaviour.

One can be aware of their jealousy but must never allow it to control their behaviour even for one second.

All humans are different and do not need to be understood but must be respected.

Respect is synonymous with love.

———————

To follow a path not chosen by thyself. To go along with someone else's idea due to an inability to say 'no'. To stay in a place because one has become so entangled, or finds it too difficult to leave, or feels sorry for the situation, or obliged, whatever the justification for weakness to act, is no way to live and will only result in resentment and unhappiness.

———————

"Truth passes through three stages: First it is ridiculed. Second, it is violently opposed. Third, it is accepted as self-evident." – A. Schopenhauer

People can change.

People can learn.

People can grow.

———————

If a heart finds harmony with another, happiness follows.

Happiness effects not only one's longevity, but their quality of life.

In short, more love equals a better life. Less love equals a worse life.

FACT: Love affects life.

———————

'An entire sea of water can't sink a ship unless it gets inside the ship. Similarly, the negativity of the world can't put you down unless you allow it to get inside you.' - G. Nasu

In times of stress, it is very common for humans to punish the ones they love, often treating strangers with more respect and kindness.

A person on the receiving end, no matter how unfortunate, must never mimic the behaviour of a stressed person. This is a very common pitfall.

If you are a happy person, stay happy.

We are all responsible for our own behaviour.

Weak people allow others to influence their mood, that is the behaviour they choose.

If one does not control their stress, their stress will control them.

––––––––––––

The number one question one should constantly ask, is 'why?'.

Why am I doing this? Why did that happen? Why do I believe what I do? Why do I believe what this person is telling me? Why do I believe what I am reading? Why is this person contacting me? Why do I allow myself to be influenced? Why am I with this person? Why am I not with that person? Why am I wasting time? Why do I procrastinate? Why do I devote my time to this? Why am I not happy? Why am I happy? Why don't I do more things that make me happy? Why do I allow people to control me? Why do I control others? Why do I not see clearly? Why do I enjoy this? Why do I not do more of what I enjoy? Why do I feel fear? Why do I only dream and not act? Why do I allow certain things to bother me? Why do I tolerate negativity? Why do I prioritise the things I do? Why do I not commit to happiness? Why do I love this person? Why does this person love me? Why waste a second? Why not live my idea of perfect? Why do I live another's idea of perfect? Why am I so stubborn to admit what I want in life and make it happen? Why do I care what others think about me? Why do I allow nonsense into my life? Etc....

And perhaps the most important 'why?'...why do I ask 'why?'...The reason is simple, to evolve.

Relying on anyone else to evolve is unintelligent and weak.

Intelligent, yet weak people, can also fall victim to this.

Strong intelligent people take responsibility for their self-evolvement.

———————

Being stubborn and going against the advice of someone else simply because it was them who made the suggestion, is unintelligent. This seems a contradiction, however, if someone makes a suggestion, question the suggestion and the source, always!

'Why did this person make such a suggestion?' 'Why does this person feel they can comfortably offer this advice freely to me?' 'Why do they believe I will listen to them?' 'Is it good advice?' Etc.

If a person has asked for advice from another, they must always remember that they do not have to act on that advice.

Advice should never be taken for being told what to do, for that would then be control, which is negative and detrimental.

There is nothing wrong with asking, listening, acting upon, and offering advice, but one must never lose sight that it's just that...advice. Always assess carefully, without simply swallowing.

Beware of people who probe with constant leading questions as they are manipulators.

People must learn to trust their instincts.

If a question feels inappropriate, it likely will be inappropriate.

Nobody is obliged to answer anyone else's questions.

Use strength, awareness, and intelligence.

One must never be a coward and answer a question out of weakness to tell a person it is none of their business.

Never feel awkward for choosing not to answer someone else's trivial, manipulative questions.

'What is your job?' 'Are you married?' 'Where do you live?' Etc…are nothing more than data gathering in order to make judgments and decide how much respect is to be afford.

If someone brings uncomfortableness to a person's life, no matter how small, it must be recognised as an attack. Defend and counter that attack, always.

Asking 'why?' more frequently, will transform a life, maximise self-esteem, and return control.

If person 'a' has control over person 'b', remember, person 'b' gave it to person 'a'.

————————

A pickpocket does not announce they are about to pick a pocket.

Like theft, successful indoctrination happens very subtly and inconspicuous.

It is indoctrination if it is accepted without open and critical analysis.

Asking the question 'why?' in many sensible ways as possible is a good method of highlighting indoctrination, as its teachers fear challenging questions.

No teacher with good intentions fears questions, on the contrary, they welcome questions.

———————

A simple test to establish honest priorities…perform the 'would I rather' test.

'Would I rather do this, or that?'

'Would I rather spend time here, or there?'

'Would I rather spend time working, or being with this person?'

'Would I rather be happy, or sad?'

'Would I rather spend my life with person, or without them?'

'Would I rather care what others think about me, or what I think about myself?'

Etc…

———————

It is easy to waste life searching to answer the question 'why are we here?'

Can we not accept that there is no answer?

The world would not miss us if we were not here. Perhaps, it would even benefit.

Can we not simply enjoy our very short time alive?

Does it make sense to hand over what limited time we have to someone else's vision and/or cause?

Does it make sense to spend even a second worshipping fictitious things of which another human invented?

Are someone else's ideas so important that they deserve our devotion and very limited time?

Is it necessary to be obedient to another and their ideas simply because one believes them to have more wisdom?

Likely, we have no real purpose, we simply live and then die, and what we do in the middle has no real significant importance.

———————

The reason transparency is so feared by people of low character, is because they understand only too well that 'knowledge is power'.

If all knowledge were to be shared openly and in real time, there would be no concentration of power, and as such, no 'master'.

We are obedient, submissive, and impressed by those we believe to have superior knowledge to us, those who know the 'secrets'. This is a low self-esteem issue.

Any time another human acts to suppress transparency, they are seeking to hold on to the power they hold over a person(s). If they refused to share completely, many would walk away, but the great manipulators that they are, understand that by 'drip feeding' their 'wisdom' at a very slow but constant rate, it is a tremendously effective method of manipulative control.

For as long as we are obedient and submissive to those we have allowed to become our very own 'masters', we are nothing more than mere peasants, and will always remain so.

Imitators can never be free.

———————

People can be creative and/or so destructive, it depends completely on their education.

How we educate, how we are educated, how we educate the educators.

Never forget that it is the educators who are responsible for good and bad.

The origins of negative beliefs and/or prejudices can always be traced back to education.

———————

The 'halo effect'. Be free of cognitive bias.

———————

If a person knew the exact date they were to die, would it make a difference to how they lived today?

The reality is that we may not know the exact date, but we do know with absolute certainty that the date exists, and every second is getting closer to that date.

Once acceptance of this fact has been afforded, perspective and understanding of what really matters in life follows, and one becomes their very own master of their very own life.

The key to a happy life lies first and foremost in love.

———————

Afterword

'Having knowledge but lacking the power to express it clearly is no better than never having any ideas at all.' - Pericles

My motivation for writing this book was to put into words, my very own personal philosophy on life. It is important to note that this is specific to me personally, and that my own life experiences and self-analysis to date, reflects how I think and act at this particular moment in time. I may think very differently tomorrow.

It is also important for any reader to understand that my philosophy is very unlikely going to be their philosophy. There is no one-size-fits-all philosophy that exists, and it is a flaw of many humans to want to impose their own ideals and ideas onto others.

Open and honest discussion of opinion is healthy, imposition of opinion is not. One must never think or act in a rigid manner or give sanction to anyone who does.

In order to discover one's very own personal and unique philosophy, it is up to each and every one of us to uncover at great depth, and at times uncomfortable honesty, who we really are and why we think and act as we do. Only the individual themself, can answer these questions, no one else.

There is possibly no more beneficial study to humanity, than the study of oneself.

'All you need is love' – Lennon/McCartney

———————

Dedicated to Persephone.

www.ingramcontent.com/pod-product-compliance
Lightning Source LLC
Chambersburg PA
CBHW060042260726
48658CB00004B/1155